# THIS BOOK BELONGS TO: